THE STOCK MARKET CRASH
BANKRUPTS AMERICA

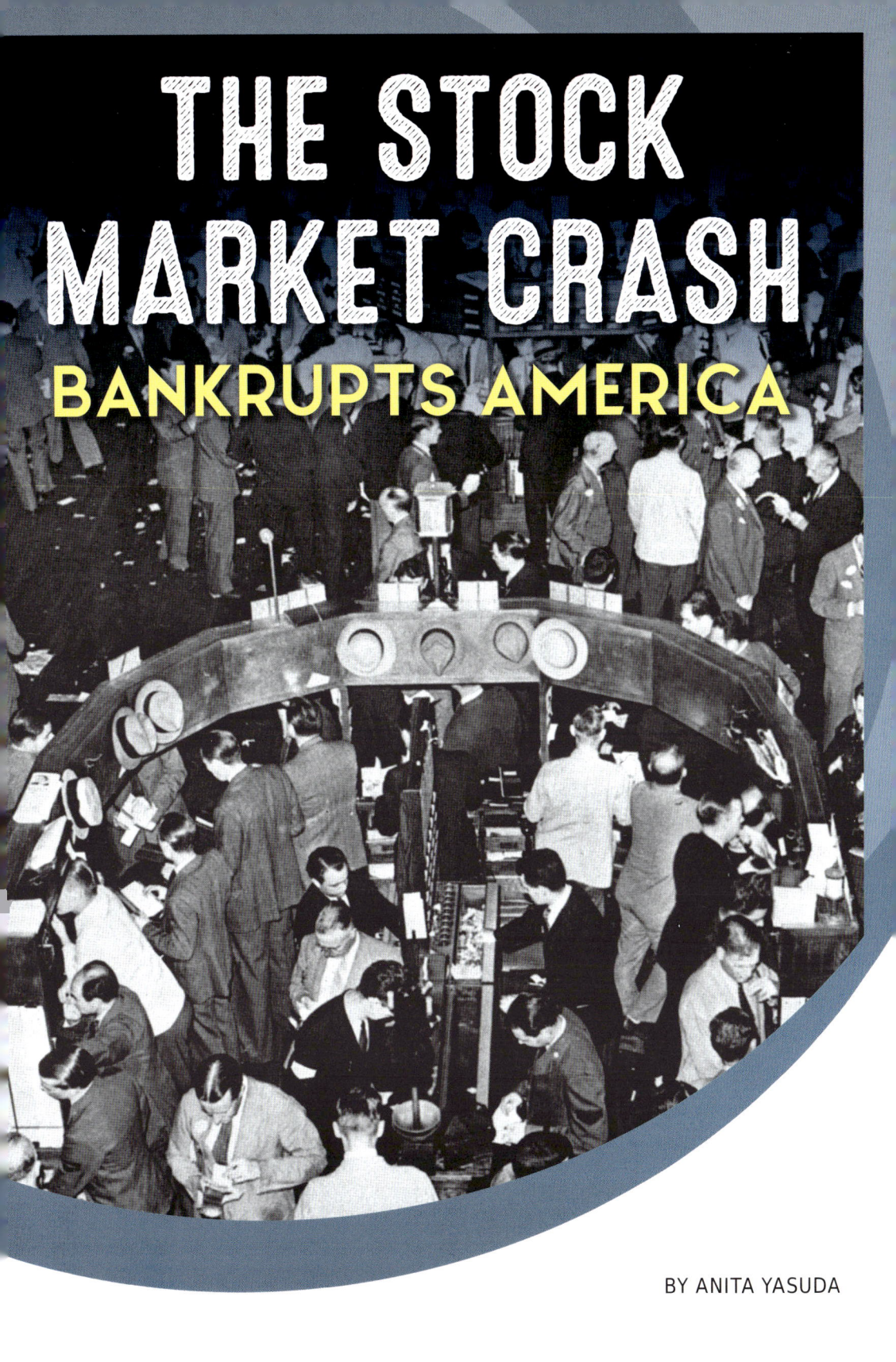

BY ANITA YASUDA

Published by The Child's World®
1980 Lookout Drive • Mankato, MN 56003-1705
800-599-READ • www.childsworld.com

Photographs ©: OFF/AFP/Getty Images, cover, 1; akg-images/Newscom, 6, 20; George Grantham Bain Collection/Library of Congress, 8; Mondadori Portfolio/Newscom, 9; AP Images, 11, 21, 25; STR/AP Images, 12; World History Archive/Newscom, 14; Underwood Archives/UIG Universal Images Group/Newscom, 16; Everett Historical/Shutterstock Images, 17, 28; Fox Photos/Hulton Archive/Getty Images, 18; Everett Collection/Newscom, 22; Harris & Ewing/Library of Congress, 27

Copyright © 2019 by The Child's World®
All rights reserved. No part of this book may be reproduced or utilized in any form or by any means without written permission from the publisher.

ISBN 9781503825239
LCCN 2017959672

Printed in the United States of America
PA02376

ABOUT THE AUTHOR

Anita Yasuda is the author of many books for young readers. Anita lives with her family in California.

TABLE OF CONTENTS

FAST FACTS AND TIMELINE 4

Chapter 1
A SURE THING 6

Chapter 2
ANXIOUS INVESTORS 12

Chapter 3
BLACK TUESDAY 18

Chapter 4
IMPACT AND CHANGE 22

Think About It 29
Glossary 30
Source Notes 31
To Learn More 32
Index 32

FAST FACTS

What was the state of the U.S. economy before the stock market crash?

- After World War I (1914–1918), the U.S. **economy** seemed healthy. Factories and cities grew larger.
- Beginning in the 1920s, more people bought goods such as radios and cars by borrowing money from places like banks. Then, people would have to pay the banks back with **interest**.

Why did people buy stocks?

- For the first time, ordinary men and women used their savings and borrowed money from the bank to buy **stocks** because the economy seemed strong. By 1929, nearly 10 percent of American families held stocks.
- From 1921 to 1928, the value of stocks mostly rose because people kept investing. People made money when their stocks went up.

What was the impact of the stock market?

- Following the crash in 1929, Americans faced hard times. This time was called the Great **Depression**.

TIMELINE

- September 3, 1929: Stock market prices reach an all-time high.

- September 5, 1929: **Economist** Roger Babson warns the public a stock market crash is coming.

- October 24, 1929: Stock prices fall as 13 million **shares** are sold. The day becomes known as Black Thursday.

- October 29, 1929: The stock market crashes when more than 16 million shares are traded. The day becomes known as Black Tuesday.

- 1930s: The United States enters an economic crisis called the Great Depression.

- March 4, 1933: Franklin D. Roosevelt becomes the 31st president of the United States. A series of government programs called the New Deal help people find work, food, and housing.

- 1939: World War II starts and the United States starts to recover from the Great Depression.

Chapter 1

A SURE THING

George Mehales leaned over his newspaper. His eyes darted up and down the stock market page. He studied it as if it was a crystal ball. Was United States Steel stock up? How about General Electric or the Radio Corporation of America? Mehales owned a restaurant in the Blue Ridge Mountains in South Carolina. He felt confident that day on October 1, 1929. He believed the stock prices did not lie.

◂ **Investors were confident they could earn money through the stock market.**

With his shares on the rise, Mehales thought of his Greek mother who sent him to live in the United States when he was younger. Perhaps she had been right. She always said he would "get rich in America someday!"[1]

With a satisfied smile, Mehales remembered that last month the stock market had reached an all-time high. Mehales folded up his newspaper. In his ears echoed economist Roger Babson's warning that "sooner or later a crash is coming."[2] Mehales didn't let Babson's statement worry him. But if Mehales had understood the truth about the economy, he would have been frightened.

The economy was stumbling as people bought less. Their wages were not keeping up with the rising price of goods. Most workers earned less than what was enough to live on. Stocks were being sold for more than they were worth. Too many people had borrowed money to play the market. This is called buying on **margin**. It allows **investors** to buy stocks that they hope to sell at a higher price. But if the stock fails, the loan plus interest must be paid back. Banks and large businesses had loaned money away. The entire financial system was as weak as a house of cards.

Irving Fisher was an economist. He lived in a large home in Connecticut. Fisher wrote many columns about the stock market.

▲ Irving Fisher taught math and economics at Yale.

In October 1929, Fisher inserted a fresh black ribbon into his typewriter to begin his latest column for the *New York Times*. His fingers jabbed at the keys until black type covered the page.

Stock prices were written on large chalkboards. ▶

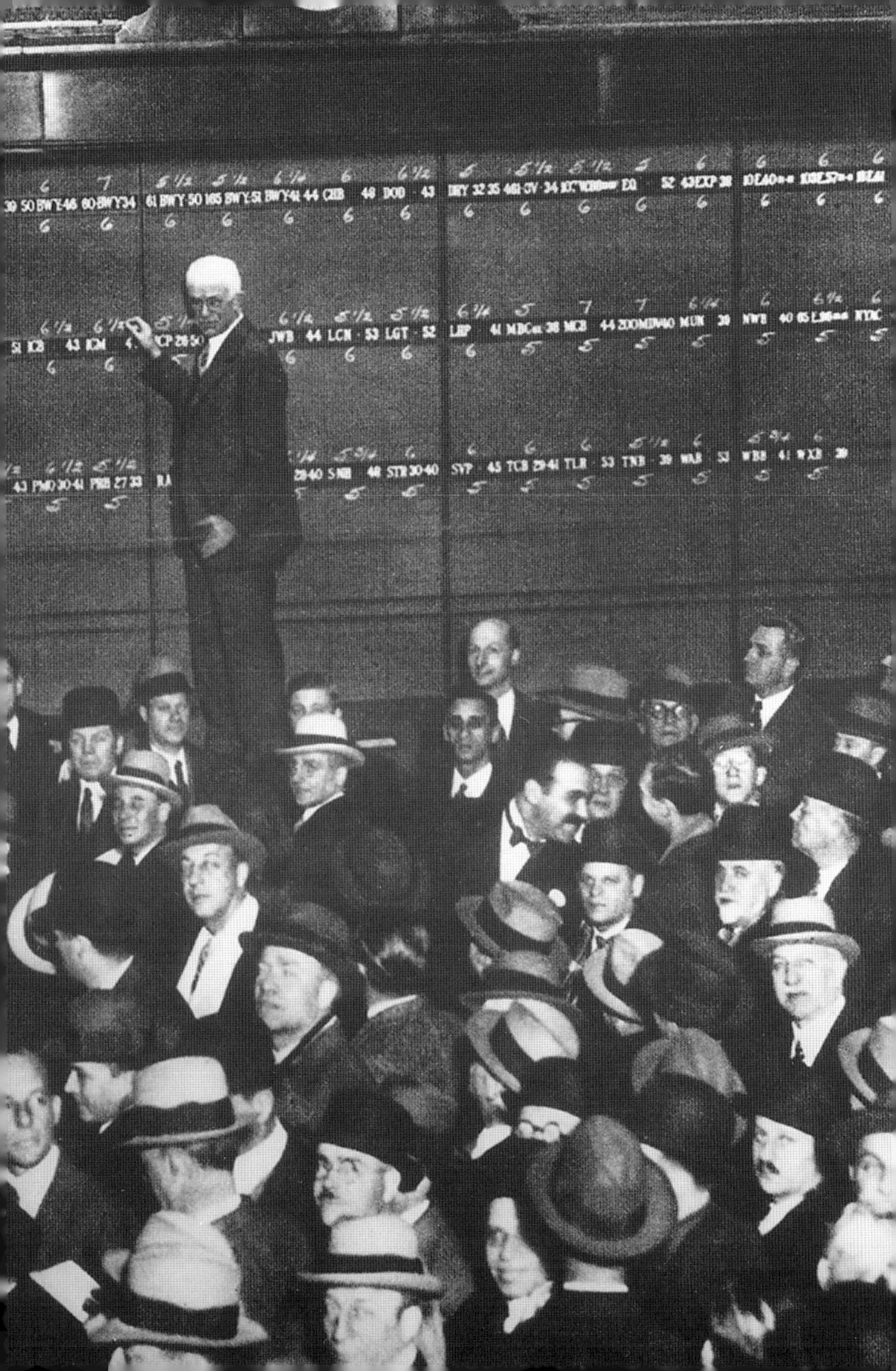

Each word explained Fisher's confidence in the stock market. He wrote, "There may be a [period of decline] in stock prices, but not anything in the nature of a crash."[3]

As Fisher carried on buying shares, ordinary Americans such as Mehales did, too. Mehales was encouraged by financial experts like Fisher. Before the sun lit his restaurant, Mehales had already devoured the experts' advice in his paper.

Many people trusted the stock market. On the streets, people shared exciting tales of drivers and maids making a fortune on the New York Stock Exchange. The stock exchange was known at that time as the Curb. One young waiter was said to have made so much money on one market tip that he quit his job. Many of these tales weren't true, but it didn't stop people from believing they could get rich quick. The stories said with only a few dollars a person might become the next Samuel Insull.

Insull went from being a poor boy in London, England, to a millionaire. It wasn't possible to turn on a light from Michigan to Texas without paying him. His electrical empire was that large. Part of his empire included the company Commonwealth Edison. He advertised his company's stock as the safest available.

Julia Walther lived in Chicago, Illinois. Everywhere she went, she heard of Insull's wealth. Walther dialed a **broker's** number.

▲ After the stock market crash, investors accused Samuel Insull (center) of stealing their money.

She bought Insull's company's stock. How could anyone lose out on investing with him?

Many people believed investing in the market was smart and safe. But on October 24, 1929, the stock market did the unthinkable. It began a dizzying spiral downward.

11

Chapter 2

ANXIOUS INVESTORS

As October marched to a close, Mehales sprang up the steps of his local bank. He wanted to keep borrowing money so he could buy more stocks. The more he bought and sold, the greater his chances were of making money. Mehales knew he should have been working in his restaurant. His sales were dropping.

◀ **Stock brokers received calls from panicked investors once the stock market began to crash.**

His **debts** were growing. Yet Mehales was too caught up in the excitement of the market. He thought that stock prices were rising. To him, it seemed as if nothing could keep their value down.

Mehales didn't realize that stocks were being sold for much more than they were worth. At this time, so many people invested that stock prices rose higher than the true value of the company. Like Mehales, these new investors were so eager to get in the stock market that they often knew little about the company whose stock they held. "I figured I could pay my debts any time," Mehales would later say. "I was making plenty of money on the market."[4]

On October 24, a loud bell sounded in the Curb in New York City, New York. It was where stock traders gathered to do business. At precisely 10:00 a.m., a great rush began. Hundreds of brokers swiftly moved over the exchange floor.

Throughout the morning, orders to sell shares came in. Voices erupted from the floor like a clash of cymbals as clerks and brokers barked orders to each other. Stock prices continued falling because of the large number of stocks that were traded.

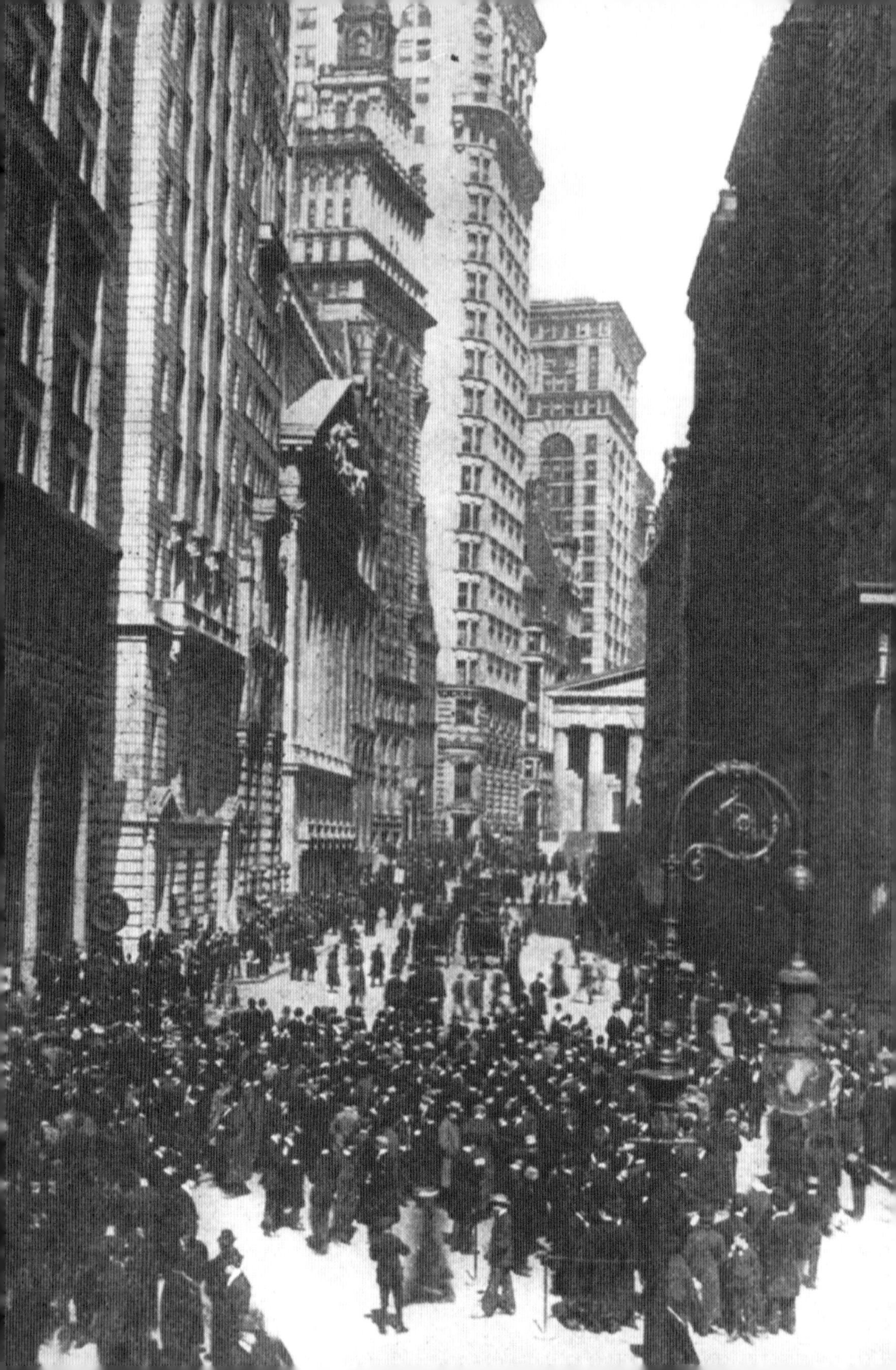

The noise in the room exploded. The roar of brokers was so loud that it spilled into the street.

By 11:00 a.m., trading had reached a frenzy. Traders yelled out their lowest offers as they scrambled to sell until their voices were hoarse, but it didn't do any good. With too few buyers, prices shot downward. Under cloudy skies, both curious and anxious people gathered under the towering columns of the Curb. Each wondered if his or her investments were safe. Every inch of pavement was filled with ashen-faced men and women, silently waiting for news. They wanted to know what was happening inside. Some had traveled to the Curb because they couldn't get through on the phone. The orders to sell had jammed the lines. People began to panic. Police arrived to keep the people calm.

As stocks went down, brokers called their clients. To hold their stocks, margin clients had to put up more money. For most margin investors, the situation was desperate. If they didn't come up with the money, brokers would sell their stocks. As Mehales listened to the voice at the other end of the phone, he steadied himself with one hand on the counter.

Mehales scrambled to secure the cash needed to keep his stocks. He contacted his brother, who sent him $1,000. Then Mehales withdrew all his savings. There was no turning back now.

◂ Hundreds of people waited outside the Curb as stock prices sank.

▲ Papers spread the news of the falling stock prices on Thursday, October 24, 1929.

So certain was his belief in the market that he would remember thinking "things would soon get better."[5] He was wrong. Almost 13 million shares had changed hands in one day. That represented a loss of approximately 14 billion dollars. The day became known as Black Thursday.

During the days following Black Thursday, the stock market looked stable once more. But many brokers were not able to go home. They needed to catch up on orders and call customers.

Then on Monday, panic set in again. A stampede of sell orders rushed over the Curb as investors dumped stocks. So many stocks changed hands that brokers worked around the clock. Some caught a few hours of rest on top of their work-strewn desks. They had their suit jackets pulled over them like blankets. These workers needed to be alert for the next day of trading. They knew there was no guarantee that the stock market would be better.

▲ Investors learned about stock prices through stock tickers.

Chapter 3

BLACK TUESDAY

On October 29, the day began with an avalanche of selling. Brokers yelled, "I'll sell, I'll sell!"[6] They shoved order slips into the Curb's 6-mile (9.7 km) network of tubes that moved mail. The tubes connected the brokers to wooden trading posts. A trading post was a permanent location where a stock was sold on the floor. Each post was staffed by a specialist who helped brokers buy or sell the stock.

◀ **Newspaper reporters at the Curb captured people's panic as stock prices fell.**

    Panicked investors wanted to get rid of stocks because prices were falling. They flooded the market with large amounts of stocks. The wild selling smashed the prices down more. One security guard who worked that day remembered that brokers "roared like a lot of lions and tigers." He said, "They clawed at one another. . . . Every once in a while . . . some poor devil collapse[d] and [fell] to the floor."[7]

    The trading could not be stopped. At noon, eight million shares had sold. The chattering of stock tickers that carried stock prices from the Curb to brokerage offices all over the United States would not stop. In one such office, Mehales paced back and forth before a domed glass ticker spitting out a stream of tape. Then, he learned the ticker was printing prices from more than an hour ago. Because the information was old, there was no way of knowing if he should buy or sell or how much his stocks were worth. Mehales's shoulders slumped as the snake-like ribbon of useless numbers coiled by his feet.

    By 3:00 p.m., the stock market had collapsed. It was the largest drop in stock prices in history. A stunning 16 million shares had been sold. The day would be called Black Tuesday.

For Mehales, his dream of making it rich in America was over. The crash had wiped him out financially. Years later he spoke about the collapse. He said the disappointment "almost killed me . . . 'cause I had nothing left. I found out what a fool I had been."[8]

In Connecticut, Irving Fisher's hand trembled as he finished a phone call and set a black phone down. His face was pale.

▲ People in San Francisco, California, tried to stay updated on the stock market crisis.

▲ Piles of ticker tape littered the floor of the Curb after the stock market crash.

He wondered how he was going to tell his wife that their $10 million fortune was gone. Fisher could no longer afford his home. Fortunately, Fisher's employer, Yale University, bought the house and rented it back to him. Fisher recognized that he had to keep teaching and writing to dig himself out from debt.

In Chicago, Julia Walther and her family suffered, too. Walther and her husband had bought stocks on margin to finance their business. They lost nearly everything. Still, she was luckier than many other people. Her family did not end up on the streets.

Chapter 4

IMPACT AND CHANGE

Out of habit, Mehales turned down the broad expanse of East Main Street in Spartanburg, South Carolina. The smell of coffee and frying bacon drew Mehales further down the street until he was standing in front of a restaurant. But Mehales couldn't force himself to go inside. The restaurant didn't belong to him anymore.

◀ Many Americans had to sell their possessions after the market crashed so they could afford basic necessities.

He hated to do it, but he had sold it at a rock-bottom price. The sale allowed him to surface from the weight of his debts. "I learned a lesson," he told a writer in 1938. "You've got to pay your debts to get along."[9] Then, Mehales started over. Years later, he was pouring refills of sweet iced tea and catching up on the local news at his new café.

Miles away in Chicago, Walther shuddered as she glanced at the *Tribune*'s headline: *Family of Nine Lives 2 Days in Abandoned Auto*. By March 1933, more than 15 million people were unemployed in the United States. With no jobs or money, long lines formed at soup kitchens. People waited for hours for a free piece of bread and a cup of soup. Many of these people had no place to live. Some of them hammered together scraps of wood, cardboard, and tin into shacks not much larger than pianos. When Walther left the safety of her apartment, she saw men by the roadside "rolled up in their overcoats, just on the pavement."[10] The sight of these men left Walther shaken. She realized that she could easily be homeless.

America was in the middle of the Great Depression. Over the crackling of static, Walther turned the dials of her radio. She heard that more than 9,000 banks were going out of business.

RATE OF UNEMPLOYMENT IN THE UNITED STATES, 1929-1939

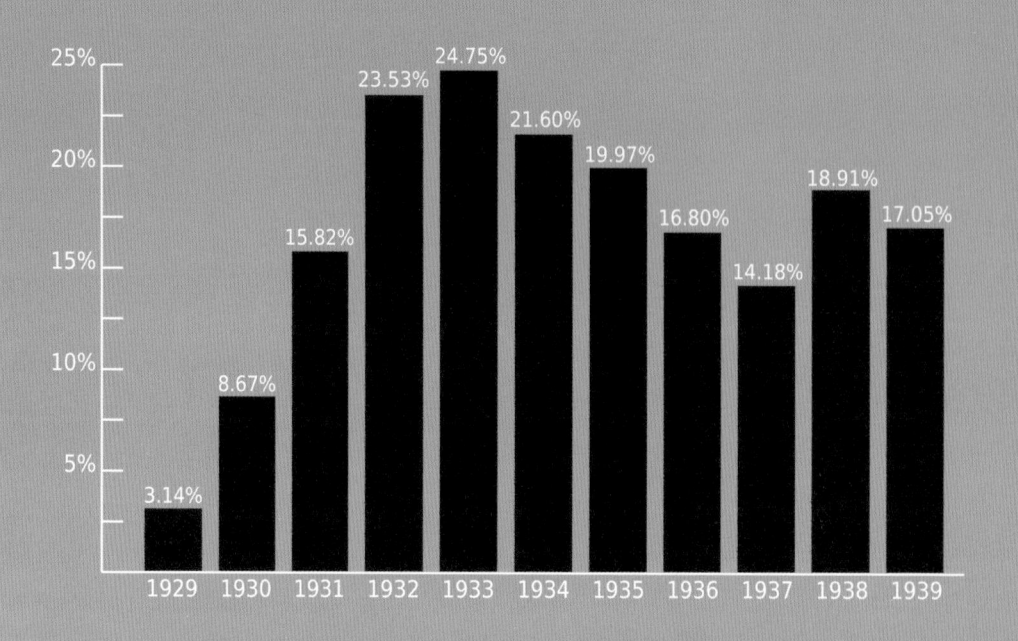

Year	Rate
1929	3.14%
1930	8.67%
1931	15.82%
1932	23.53%
1933	24.75%
1934	21.60%
1935	19.97%
1936	16.80%
1937	14.18%
1938	18.91%
1939	17.05%

Some banks had invested in the stock market. Other banks lost money when people's debts were left unpaid. Walther knew some people who lost all their savings once their bank closed.

▶ Many people relied on soup kitchens to provide them with meals during the Great Depression.

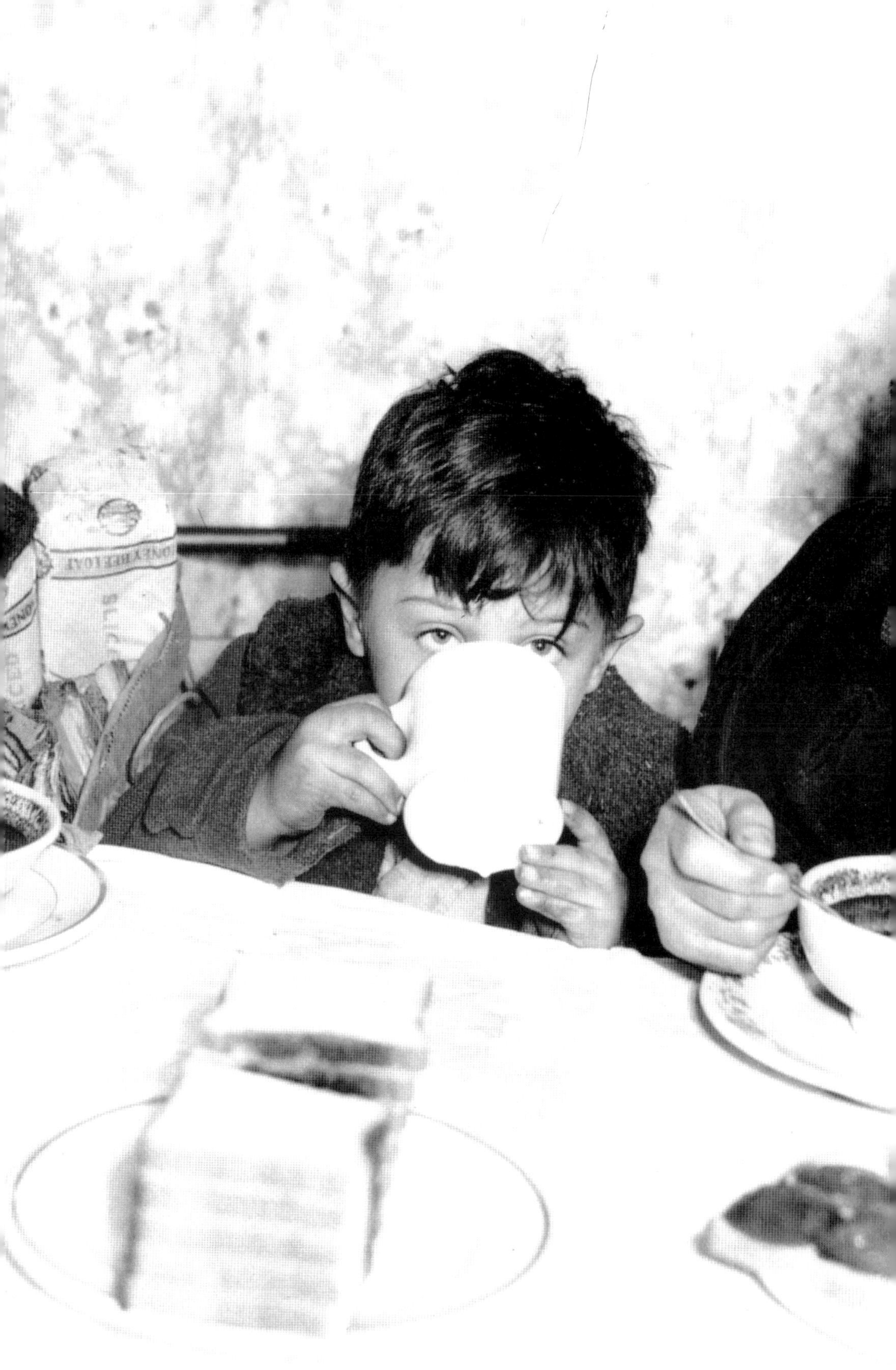

Walther's radio also brought her reports of fierce dust storms from Texas to Nebraska. Crops couldn't grow in that weather. Without crops, thousands of farm families were tossed from their land when they couldn't pay their bills.

Americans were ready for a change. Under a gray sky in 1933, a huge crowd cheered as Franklin D. Roosevelt was sworn in as president. The new government sent out scientists and engineers to choose spots to build bridges, dams, and roads. During radio speeches from the White House, Roosevelt explained that these projects would put people to work. Today, people still use thousands of those structures. One example is the massive Hoover Dam that curves along the Arizona-Nevada border. Roosevelt's government also passed programs to help the unemployed, farmers, and the elderly. One of these programs was the Social Security Act. This act still provides for people today. Elderly people receive money each month when they no longer work. In addition, if people lose their jobs they receive financial help from the government.

Roosevelt wanted to protect people from banking failures. So he created the Federal Deposit Insurance Corporation (FDIC). Now, if a bank closes its doors, people will not lose their savings.

During the first three months of Franklin D. Roosevelt's ▶ presidency, many laws were passed to help struggling Americans.

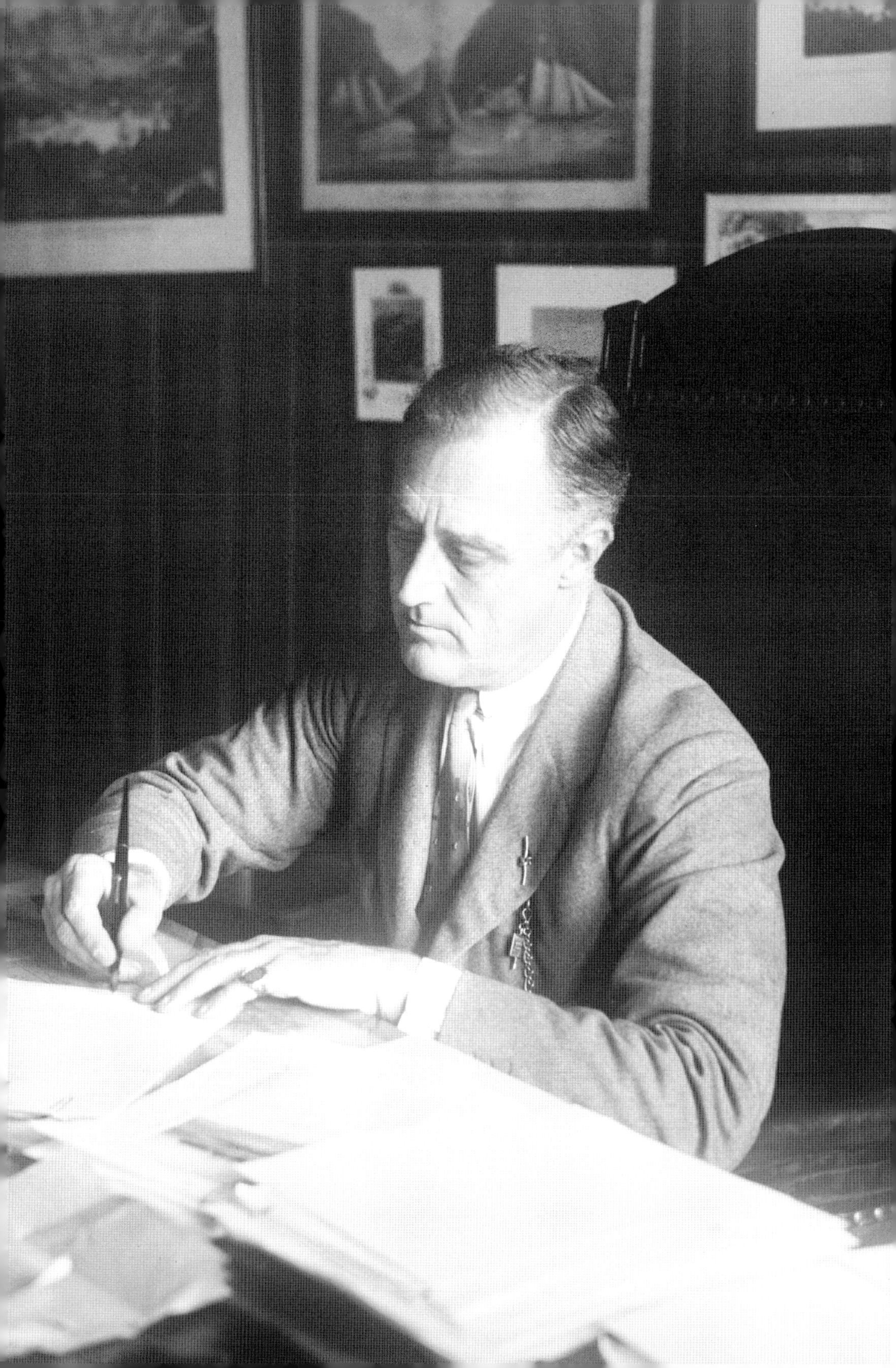

▲ During the Great Depression, people went on marches to demand jobs.

In addition, the government set up the Securities and Exchange Commission (SEC). The SEC watches out for people who invest their money. All businesses or people who sell or buy stocks must register with the SEC.

There were no programs in place in 1929 to help people affected by the stock market crash. Today, millions of Americans are protected by these laws. When customers put money in their accounts, they know the money will be there. Before people buy or sell stocks, they can research the companies traded on the stock exchange. This helps people make informed decisions.

THINK ABOUT IT

- In the 1920s, many Americans bought stocks. They believed they would get rich quickly. Why were people willing to risk their savings for the slim chance of getting rich?
- In the years after the crash, how did the daily lives of ordinary people change? If the stock market crashed today, how do you think your life would change?
- Franklin D. Roosevelt wanted to help poor, homeless, and unemployed Americans. If you worked in the government during the Great Depression, how would you have helped improve the lives of people in the United States?

GLOSSARY

broker (BROH-ker): A broker is a person who buys or sells stocks for a customer. George Mehales owed money to his broker.

debts (DETZ): Debts occur when people or businesses owe money that they borrowed. George Mehales had many debts because he borrowed money to buy stocks.

depression (di-PRESH-uhn): A depression is a period of time when there are fewer jobs and people spend less. Millions of Americans had no work during the Great Depression.

economist (i-KON-uh-mist): A person who studies how money moves between people, banks, and businesses is called an economist. Irving Fisher was an economist who lectured at Yale University.

economy (i-KON-uh-mee): The economy is how people, businesses, or the government manage their money and resources. Before the stock market crash, the U.S. economy seemed strong.

interest (IN-trest): Interest is a fee for using someone else's money. A bank charges interest for borrowing money.

investors (in-VES-torz): Investors buy something in hopes of selling it in the future for more money. Julia Walther and George Mehales were investors in the stock market.

margin (MAR-juhn): A margin is a down payment to buy a stock or stocks. George Mehales's stock prices fell below his margin.

shares (SHAIRZ): Shares are a partial ownership in a company. Many people sold their shares on Black Tuesday.

stocks (STOKS): Stocks are pieces of paper showing ownership issued by a company in return for money. Julia Walther bought stocks.

SOURCE NOTES

1. "George Mehales." *Library of Congress.* Library of Congress, n.d. Web. 15 Nov. 2017.

2. John Kenneth Galbraith. *The Great Crash, 1929.* Boston, MA: Houghton Mifflin Harcourt, 2009. Print. 84.

3. Ibid. 88.

4. "George Mehales." *Library of Congress.* Library of Congress, n.d. Web. 15 Nov. 2017.

5. Ibid.

6. "The Wall Street Crash of 1929: How the Daily Express Reported It 85 Years Ago." *Express.* Express, 10 Oct. 2014. Web. 15 Nov. 2017.

7. "The Hoover Story Gallery 6: The Great Depression." *Herbert Hoover Presidential Library and Museum.* Herbert Hoover Presidential Library and Museum, n.d. Web. 15 Nov. 2017.

8. "George Mehales." *Library of Congress.* Library of Congress, n.d. Web. 15 Nov. 2017.

9. Ibid.

10. Studs Terkel. *Hard Times: An Oral History of the Great Depression.* New York, NY: New Press, 2000. Print. 190–193.

TO LEARN MORE

Books

Karlitz, Gail. *Growing Money: A Complete Investing Guide for Kids.* New York, NY: Price Stern Sloan, 2010.

McDaniel, Melissa. *The Great Depression.* New York, NY: Children's Press, 2012.

Mullenbach, Cheryl. *The Great Depression for Kids: Hardship and Hope in 1930s America.* Chicago, IL: Chicago Review Press, 2015.

Web Sites

Visit our Web site for links about the Stock Market Crash: childsworld.com/links

Note to Parents, Teachers, and Librarians: We routinely verify our Web links to make sure they are safe and active sites. So encourage your readers to check them out!

INDEX

banks, 4, 7, 12, 23, 24, 26
Black Thursday, 5, 16
Black Tuesday, 5, 19
brokers, 10, 13, 15, 16, 17, 18, 19
Commonwealth Edison, 10
Curb, the, 10, 13, 15, 17, 18, 19
debts, 13, 21, 23, 24
economy, 4, 7

Fisher, Irving, 7, 8, 10, 20, 21
Great Depression, 4, 5, 23, 24
Hoover Dam, 26
Insull, Samuel, 10, 11
interest, 4, 7
loans, 7
Mehales, George, 6, 7, 10, 12, 13, 15, 16, 19, 20, 22, 23

Roosevelt, Franklin D., 5, 26
savings, 4, 15, 24, 26
Social Security Act, 26
stock prices, 5, 6, 10, 13, 15, 19
Walther, Julia, 10, 11, 21, 23, 24, 26
Yale University, 21

32